D1294782

Spooky Schools

by Natalie Lunis

Consultant: Troy Taylor
President of the American Ghost Society

BEARPORT
PUBLISHING

New York, New York

Credits

Cover and Title Page, © pzAxe/Shutterstock, Lisa F. Young/Shutterstock, and Ferenc Szelepcsenyi/Shutterstock; 4–5, Kim Jones; 6, © Sara Bogush; 7, © Elyse Eidelheit/FlickrVision; 8B, © Fay Ratta; 8TL, © Matt Pasant; 9BL, © Copyright Bettmann/Corbis/AP Images; 9BR, © Lebrecht Music and Arts Photo Library/Alamy; 10, © Nicholas P. Vinacco; 11, © Time & Life Pictures/Getty Images; 12, © James Caldwell/Alamy; 13, © State Archives of Florida, Florida Memory; 14, © Augusta State University; 15T, © Adam Smith; 15M, © Chris Thelen/The Augusta Chronicle/ZUMAPRESS.com; 15B, © Chris Thelen/The Augusta Chronicle/ZUMAPRESS.com; 16, © Chriscobar; 17T, © Old Visuals/Alamy; 17B, © The Ram Archives; 18, © Jared C. Benedict; 19BL, © Erich Hartmann/Magnum Photos; 19BR, © Hachette Book Group, Inc.; 20, © Brian Gray Photography; 21T, © Paul A. Souders/CORBIS; 21B, © Russell Underwood/CORBIS; 22, © Diana Cheng/FlickrVision; 23, © Pokaz/Shutterstock; 24, © Los Angeles Public Library Photo Collection; 25, © Tomas Rodriguez/Corbis; 26, © C03705, Austin History Center, Austin Public Library; 27, © Chamille White/Shutterstock; 31, © Perutskyi Petro/Shutterstock.

Publisher: Kenn Goin
Editorial Director: Adam Siegel
Creative Director: Spencer Brinker
Design: Dawn Beard Creative
Photo Researcher: Picture Perfect Professionals, LLC

Library of Congress Cataloging-in-Publication Data

Lunis, Natalie.
  Spooky schools / by Natalie Lunis.
      p. cm. (Scary places)
  Includes bibliographical references (p.   ) and index.
  ISBN-13: 978-1-61772-750-4 (library binding)
  ISBN-10: 1-61772-750-4 (library binding)
  1. Haunted universities and colleges—Juvenile literature. 2. Haunted schools—Juvenile literature.
3. Haunted places—Juvenile literature. 4. Ghosts—Juvenile literature. I. Title.
  BF1478.L86 2013
  133.1'22—dc23
                                    2012040428

Copyright © 2013 Bearport Publishing Company, Inc. All rights reserved. No part of this publication may be reproduced in whole or in part, stored in any retrieval system, or transmitted in any form or by any means, electronic, mechanical, photocopying, recording, or otherwise, without written permission from the publisher.

For more information, write to Bearport Publishing Company, Inc., 45 West 21st Street, Suite 3B, New York, New York 10010. Printed in the United States of America.

10 9 8 7 6 5 4 3 2 1

Contents

Spooky Schools

Most of the time schools aren't so scary. Usually they are just buildings filled with students studying in classrooms, reading in the library, playing in the gym, and eating in the lunchroom. Imagine how truly scary the school day would be, though, if there were ghosts in attendance.

Within the 11 spooky schools in this book, you'll meet many different ghosts. Among them are a girl who preferred wandering in a beautiful garden to life in the big city, a high school student who drowned in a pool and now reaches out to swimmers there, and a famous playwright who continues to inspire college students—not only through his work but also by sharing a building with them. All of these **spirits** are so eager to be in school that they have decided to stay around forever.

The Ghost in the Garden

Bard College, Annandale-on-Hudson, New York

Students at Bard College are lucky to go to school on a gardenlike **campus** overlooking the Hudson River. The spot is so beautiful that one girl, it seems, decided to return to it after death—and hasn't left since.

In 1899, Captain Andrew C. Zabriskie bought a large piece of property overlooking the Hudson River. There, he built a grand white **mansion** to use as a summer home for his family. He also put in beautiful gardens and walkways, many with breathtaking views of the river. Because the property had been formerly known as Blithewood, everyone called the new house Blithewood Mansion.

Blithewood Mansion

Just over fifty years later, in 1951, the captain's son gave Blithewood Mansion to nearby Bard College. Since then, students and teachers have seen a strange girl wandering both outside and inside the house, which is now used by **professors** who teach **economics**.

The girl, who seems to be somewhere between eight and twelve years old, is believed to be Captain Zabriskie's daughter. People say that one winter night she fell—or perhaps jumped—to her death from a window of her family's New York City apartment. Because she disliked the big city, she is now reported to spend all her time as a ghost at her family's beautiful home on the river.

A view of the gardens

Captain Zabriskie had four statues of his daughter made for the gardens at Blithewood. Three of the statues remain, while there is only an empty spot where the fourth statue once stood. Some say that the young girl haunts the garden by wandering the grounds in the form of this statue.

The Haunted Library

Baylor University, Waco, Texas

Elizabeth Barrett Browning (1806–1861) is a famous English poet. She never set foot in the United States, yet her ghost is said to haunt the library of a university in Texas. Why?

Baylor University

Inside the Armstrong Browning Library at Baylor University

8

As a young woman, Elizabeth Barrett was often ill. She spent her days in her bedroom in her family's home in London writing letters and poetry. Her life changed in 1845, however, when another young poet, named Robert Browning, visited her there.

During their first meeting, Robert told her how much he loved her poems. A year later, he and Elizabeth married and moved to Italy. There, the two lived happily, often working side by side, until Elizabeth's death in 1861.

Almost a hundred years later, a professor of English at Baylor University in Waco, Texas, helped the school build a large collection of the Brownings' letters and **manuscripts**. The school also collected furniture, paintings, and jewelry that had belonged to the poets and built a beautiful library to hold the items. Today, people who spend time in the building say that Elizabeth's ghost can be found there as well. Some think that she cannot stay away from the belongings and writings that meant so much to her. Others recall that in one of her most famous poems, Elizabeth declares that she will love her husband even more after death. Does she keep her promise by forever searching for him?

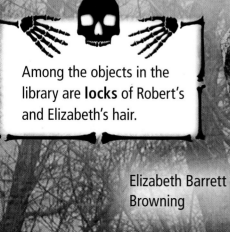

Among the objects in the library are **locks** of Robert's and Elizabeth's hair.

Elizabeth Barrett Browning

Robert Browning

A Playwright's Comeback

Boston University, Boston, Massachusetts

While in college, many students study the work of famous writers from the past. Some students at a large school in the heart of Boston get to do even more—they live with one.

In some ways, Shelton Hall is like any other college **dormitory**. The students there spend their time studying, hanging out with friends, listening to music, and doing laundry and other day-to-day tasks.

Shelton Hall

SHELTON HALL

In other ways, however, Shelton Hall is different from other student housing. Up on the fourth floor, the elevator often stops for no reason at all. There are knocks on the doors—even though no one is out in the hallway. Sometimes at night, a strong wind blows down the hall.

Surprisingly, the students who live in Shelton Hall have an explanation for the strange events. Before the building became a dormitory, it was the Shelton Hotel. For two years, Eugene O'Neill, one of America's greatest playwrights, lived in a room on the fourth floor. He also died there in 1953. Since then, people claim he has been haunting the hallway. His presence has not scared young people away, however. In fact, it has done the opposite. The fourth floor—now known as the Writers' **Corridor**—attracts writing students who hope to become better at their craft by meeting up with O'Neill's spirit.

Students put up a bulletin board in the fourth-floor hallway so that they can post notes about the strange things they have seen. So far, O'Neill's ghost has not added any messages of his own.

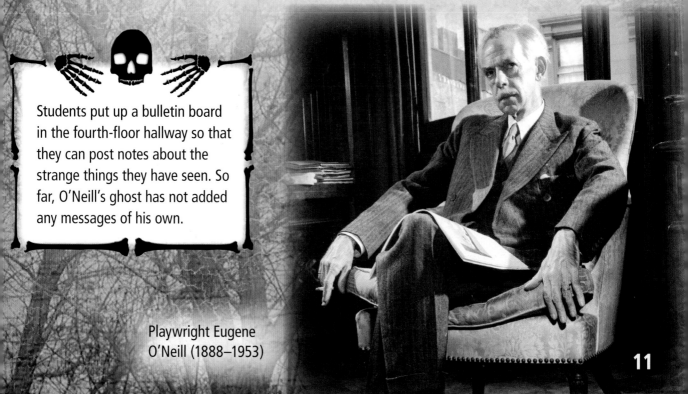

Playwright Eugene O'Neill (1888–1953)

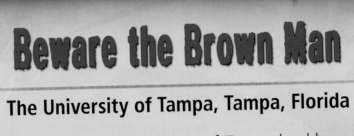

Beware the Brown Man

The University of Tampa, Tampa, Florida

Students who attend the University of Tampa lead busy lives. A little more than a hundred years ago, however, people came to the same spot to relax and have fun. At least one of them might still be coming back—unaware of the changes that have taken place since that time.

The University of Tampa

Even though they have never seen him, most students at the University of Tampa know all about a strange person who could not possibly belong at the school. Why? According to those who have spotted him, the man is unforgettable. He wears an old-fashioned, brown three-piece suit and has glowing red eyes. He also appears and disappears suddenly on a stairway.

Because of his clothing, the figure has become known as the Brown Man. The strange man's suit also offers a clue to whom he might be and why he might sometimes show up on campus. Before the property in downtown Tampa became the site of the school, it was known as the Tampa Bay Hotel. Photos from the late 1800s show the hotel's beautiful and spacious lobby. They also show a group of men talking and relaxing on a high-ceilinged porch. Could the Brown Man be one of them—a ghost who returns in an attempt to relive the good times of the past?

The hotel's porch

Ghostly sounds have also reminded students of the school's past as a hotel. In one area, some people have heard the squeaking wheels of food carts. In another area, where a **casino** once stood, some have heard the sound of rolling dice.

An Unhappy Ending

Augusta State University, Augusta, Georgia

At a school in Georgia, two ghostly voices are heard sharply disagreeing. What are these troubled spirits arguing about? Why have they been unable to find peace so many years after their deaths?

In 1861, America's northern and southern states were fighting the **Civil War**. Twenty-one-year-old Emily Galt was engaged to a young man, but the two could not stay together. The young man had decided to go off and join the **Confederate Army**. No matter how much Emily argued and pleaded with him, he refused to change his mind. He went to war, and Emily's worst fears came true—he was killed in battle.

Augusta State University

Emily's home—the place where she and the young man argued—later became part of Augusta State University. Those who work and study in the building, known today as Bellevue Hall, have heard two people arguing, even though the couple could never be found.

Bellevue Hall—the building where the sharp disagreements are heard

Students and **faculty** have also seen Emily's name etched on the glass of a second-floor window. According to the stories that are told on campus, Emily used her diamond **engagement ring** to scratch the letters in the windowpane. Shortly after she learned of her **fiancé**'s death, she threw herself from the window. Ever since, she and the young man seem unable to stop repeating the upsetting last moments they had together.

The window on which Emily's name is etched

Other strange activity also suggests that Emily's former home is haunted. Phones sometimes ring for no reason and doors open and close. A television is also said to turn itself on and off.

A close-up view of Emily's name scratched into the window

15

Touched by Death

Fordham University, Bronx, New York

College students are usually young and healthy. So why do those who live in a beautiful old dormitory sometimes feel as if they are surrounded by death?

With its tall trees and castlelike buildings that cast long shadows in the late afternoon, Fordham University looks like a place that might be haunted. In fact, many people say that there are several spots on campus that are visited by ghosts. Perhaps the scariest of these is a dormitory called Finlay Hall.

Fordham University

In the early 1900s, Finlay Hall did not serve as a home for students, as it does today. Instead, the building held a medical school—with a **morgue** filled with dead bodies in the basement. Those who live in Finlay now believe that this fact explains why they sometimes wake up with the feeling that an icy hand is grabbing their throat.

The building's past may also explain why in a few especially large rooms that have **lofts**, students sometimes wake up and see a group of ghostly faces staring down at them. As everyone in Finlay Hall knows, the balcony-like structures were the place where medical students once stood as they observed professors and more advanced students cut into **corpses** in order to learn about the human body.

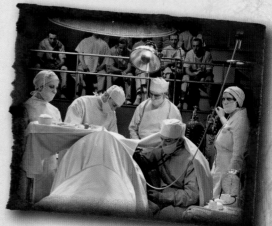

Medical students watch doctors perform an operation.

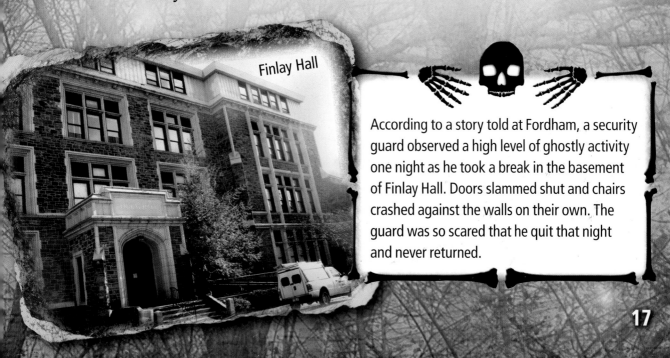

Finlay Hall

According to a story told at Fordham, a security guard observed a high level of ghostly activity one night as he took a break in the basement of Finlay Hall. Doors slammed shut and chairs crashed against the walls on their own. The guard was so scared that he quit that night and never returned.

Haunted in Fact and Fiction

Bennington College, Bennington, Vermont

In the late 1950s, author Shirley Jackson wrote a novel called *The Haunting of Hill House*. The book became one of the most famous horror stories ever written. Although it is fiction, Jackson's work was based on a very real house that belonged to the college that was just down the street from her home.

Jennings Hall at Bennington College

Jennings Hall is a forty-room house that in 1939 became Bennington College's music building. Music classes are held there, and students use small practice rooms to play the piano or violin or to work on their singing. The sounds of music are not the only ones that are heard in this beautiful New England mansion, however. People have reported hearing footsteps and whispers inside—even though no one was around to make these noises.

In 1945, Shirley Jackson came to Bennington because her husband had been hired to teach there. The young couple's house was quite close to Jennings Hall. It is believed that the stories about the building and the strange happenings inside gave Jackson the idea for her own haunted house book.

It is also almost certain that Jackson, like other people at Bennington, thought that the building became even spookier in 1946. During that year, a music student named Paula Welden disappeared. She was last seen heading out of town. Did she run away or was she murdered—only to return to Jennings Hall as a ghost? To this day, no one knows what really happened to her.

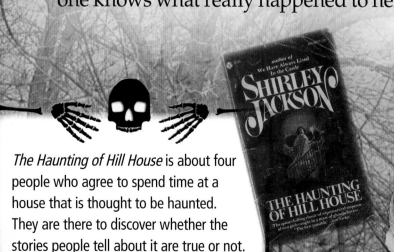

The Haunting of Hill House is about four people who agree to spend time at a house that is thought to be haunted. They are there to discover whether the stories people tell about it are true or not.

Author Shirley Jackson (1916–1965)

A Deadly Promise

Kenyon College, Gambier, Ohio

More than a hundred years ago, a college student in Ohio died while proving his trust in his schoolmates. Today, students turn out every year to show that although he is gone, he is not forgotten.

Kenyon College

On October 28, 1905, Stuart Pierson was at college, preparing himself for a test. He was not about to take an exam in math or science or history, however. Instead, he wanted to show that he was willing to place complete trust in the members of a **fraternity** called Delta Kappa Epsilon—or DKE for short. If he passed the test, the fraternity brothers would allow him to join their club and live in their house on campus.

Stuart did as he was told. He followed a group of students to a train **trestle** and lay down on the tracks. The students instructed him to stay there until they returned. When they came back, they were in for a shock. A train had unexpectedly come through and killed Stuart.

Since then, Stuart is remembered every year on the **anniversary** of his death. Members of DKE carry a coffin filled with stones to the spot where he died. Stuart is also said to appear on that day. People claim they have seen him looking out of a window on the fourth floor of the fraternity house— finally at home in the building where he had wanted to live.

Stuart—called "Stuey" and "Stu" by students at Kenyon—also haunts the DKE house at other times of the year. Windows open and close, and his footsteps are sometimes heard on the top floor.

Trouble in the Bell Tower

San Francisco Art Institute, San Francisco, California

What would you expect to hear in an old bell tower? Most people would say the deep, rich clanging of a bell. Yet that's not what those who have been inside the bell tower of a famous art school would say. According to them, what stands out is the sound of unhappy ghosts!

The San Francisco Art Institute

In 1947, Bill Morehouse was a student at the Art Institute of San Francisco. To help make ends meet, he took a job as a night watchman and decided to sleep in the Institute's bell tower. Starting on his first night, strange noises made him wonder if someone—or something—else was there as well. As he lay in bed, he heard footsteps coming up the tower's staircase. Then he heard a door open. More sounds made him think someone was passing through his room and then turning around and closing the door.

For a long time, Bill continued to hear the footsteps. Later, other strange events occurred, adding to people's belief that the school was haunted. For example, in a sculpture studio one night, all the power tools turned on by themselves. Finally, a team of **psychics** was called in. One of them saw an image of a graveyard—suggesting that spirits who had been disturbed were the source of the troubles. Research later proved that the school had in fact been built on the grounds of an old cemetery.

Some of the psychics who investigated the school had a different idea. They thought that the haunting was caused by the spirits of art students who were not able to produce the great artwork that they had hoped to create.

Afraid of the Water

Ramona Convent Secondary School, Alhambra, California

Often, there is more than one ghost at work in a place that is truly haunted. That is the case at one high school in California. At least three different ghosts are said to roam through different parts of the 110-year-old campus.

Ramona Convent
Secondary School

Ramona **Convent** Secondary School is one of the oldest high schools in California. So it is not surprising that this all-girls school is home to more than one ghost—or at least more than one ghost story.

According to reports, the ghostly figure of a nun has been seen throughout the school. White and glowing, the spirit floats from room to room and is most often seen in the library. Another spirit is not seen at all. Instead, it is heard in the form of piano playing. The music fills the air, even though there is no one around who could be causing it.

The most frightening ghost of all haunts the school's swimming pool. People say that a girl accidentally drowned there. They also say that since that tragic event, swimmers have sometimes felt someone pulling on their leg from underneath the water— as if trying to ask for help. Reportedly, some students are so frightened when they hear the story that they refuse to go in the pool.

In 1987, an earthquake damaged several buildings at the school. People say that that is roughly the same time when the stories of the ghostly piano playing and the haunted pool began. Is it possible that the ghosts were disturbed by the shaking of the earth as well?

Voices from the Past

Metz Elementary School, Austin, Texas

Can a school be haunted by all the students who have gone there in the past? That's what people in one Texas community asked themselves not long ago. As they prepared to knock down a school that had been closed, the building itself acted up like an angry ghost—giving new meaning to the expression "school spirit."

Metz Elementary School before it was demolished

Metz Elementary School was built in 1916. By the 1980s, however, the building where its classes were held had become too small. More children than ever lived in the community, and so a bigger school was needed.

When the **demolition** of the old building began in 1990, members of the construction crew noticed many strange things. Their watches stopped. Their equipment broke down. Ladders shook when workers tried to climb them. Most frighteningly of all, the laughter of children was heard coming from the walls, and writing appeared on the school's chalkboards.

Because of these events, workers began to quit. Then a wall collapsed, killing one crew member. The job was finally completed—although it took six months longer than it was supposed to. Today, even though the school no longer stands, it still lives on through the stories that people tell about its haunted past.

According to some reports, one of the workers from the demolition crew dug up a tree from the school's yard. He then planted it in the front yard of his daughter's house. Afterward, people could hear children's voices when they came near the tree.

Kenyon College
Gambier, Ohio
A test of trust turns deadly.

Bennington College
Bennington, Vermont
Ghostly music students inspire a writer of horror fiction.

San Francisco Art Institute
San Francisco, California
A bell tower is haunted by restless spirits.

Ramona Convent Secondary School
Alhambra, California
Spirits haunt the halls while a ghostly swimmer waits in the pool.

Baylor University
Waco, Texas
A famous poet remains with her writings and belongings—even after her death.

Metz Elementary School
Austin, Texas
A haunted building fights back when workers try to tear it down.

The University of Tampa
Tampa, Florida
A figure from the past who wears a brown suit and has glowing red eyes haunts today's students.

Augusta State University
Augusta, Georgia
A young woman forever begs her fiancé not to go to war.

Around the World

Arctic Ocean

NORTH AMERICA

EUROPE

ASIA

Atlantic Ocean

AFRICA

Pacific Ocean

SOUTH AMERICA

Indian Ocean

AUSTRALIA

Southern Ocean

ANTARCTICA

Boston University
Boston, Massachusetts

A famous playwright haunts the halls of a dormitory that was once a hotel.

Bard College
Annandale-on-Hudson, New York

A ghost haunts a beautiful garden—possibly in the form of a statue.

Fordham University
Bronx, New York

Students live in a place where dead bodies were once stored—and studied.

Glossary

anniversary (an-uh-VUR-suh-ree) a date that marks something that happened on the same day in the past

campus (KAM-puhss) the land and building or buildings that make up a school

casino (kuh-SEE-noh) a place where people gamble by playing cards and other kinds of games

Civil War (SIV-il WOR) the U.S. war between the southern states and the northern states, which lasted from 1861–1865

Confederate Army (*kuhn*-FED-ur-uht ARM-ee) the army that fought for the southern states during the Civil War

convent (KON-vuhnt) a place where nuns live and work

corpses (KORPS-iz) dead bodies

corridor (KOR-uh-dur) a hallway

demolition (*dem*-uh-LISH-uhn) the knocking down of a building or other structure

dormitory (DOR-muh-*tor*-ee) a building with rooms where students live and sleep on a college campus

economics (*eh*-kuh-NOM-iks) the study of how goods are bought and sold

engagement ring (in-GAYJ-muhnt RING) a ring given by one person to another to show that the couple is going to get married

faculty (FAK-uhl-tee) teachers in a school or college

fiancé (fee-AHN-say) the man whom a woman is going to marry

fraternity (fruh-TURN-i-tee) a group of students who form a club and live together at a college

locks (LOKS) curls of hair

lofts (LOFTS) spaces that are inside rooms and are raised up toward the roof or ceiling

mansion (MAN-shuhn) a very large and grand house

manuscripts (MAN-yoo-skripts) books that are written by hand

morgue (MORG) a place where dead bodies are kept before being buried

professors (pruh-FESS-urz) people who teach at colleges or universities

psychics (SYE-kiks) people who can communicate with the spirits of the dead

spirits (SPIHR-its) supernatural creatures, such as a ghosts

trestle (TRESS-uhl) a bridge that holds up something, such as railroad tracks

Bibliography

Austin, Joanne. *Weird Hauntings: True Tales of Ghostly Places*. New York: Sterling (2006).

Hauck, Dennis William. *Haunted Places: The National Directory*. New York: Penguin Books (2002).

Mott, Allan S. *Haunted Schools*. Edmonton, Canada: Ghost House Books (2003).

Steiger, Brad. *Real Ghosts, Restless Spirits, and Haunted Places*. Canton, MI: Visible Ink Press (2003).

Read More

Lunis, Natalie. *Haunted Caves (Scary Places)*. New York: Bearport (2012).

Parvis, Sarah. *Haunted Hotels (Scary Places)*. New York: Bearport (2008).

Williams, Dinah. *Spooky Cemeteries (Scary Places)*. New York: Bearport (2008).

Zullo, Allan. *Haunted Schools: True Ghost Stories*. New York: Scholastic (2004).

Learn More Online

To learn more about spooky schools, visit
www.bearportpublishing.com/ScaryPlaces

Index

About the Author

Natalie Lunis has written many nonfiction books for children. She lives in New York's lower Hudson River Valley—the home of the Headless Horseman.